Bugs

Rosie Dickins

Designed by

Catherine-Anne MacKinnon and Lucy Owen

Illustrated by John Woodcock

Additional design work by Cristina Adami and Neil Francis

Consultant: Dr. Margaret Rostron

Series editor: Gillian Doherty

Contents

Internet links

For links to the websites recommended in this book, go to the **Usborne Quicklinks Website** at www.usborne-quicklinks.com and enter the keywords "discovery bugs". Usborne Publishing is not responsible for the content on any website other than its own. Please read the Internet safety guidelines on the Usborne Quicklinks Website and on page 47 of this book.

★ Pictures in this book with a star symbol beside them can be downloaded for your own personal use from the Usborne Quicklinks Website.

Cover picture: close-up of a cicada
Title page: tailor ants on a leaf
This page: a tropical birdwing butterfly feeding on a flower

What is a bug?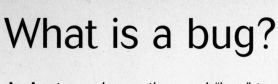

Most people use the word "bug" to mean all sorts of creepy-crawlies, from beetles and flies to spiders and centipedes. There are well over a million different kinds, or species, of bugs. Of all the animal species we know about, around three-quarters are bugs.

This dragonfly is an arthropod. It belongs to the group of arthropods called insects.

Bug groups

Scientists divide living creatures into groups according to their features. The creatures most people describe as "bugs" all belong to a group called arthropods. Arthropods have a hard covering on their bodies and have six or more legs. You can tell different kinds of bugs apart by counting their legs.

Insects

Bugs with six legs are called insects. For example, beetles, butterflies and bees are all insects. Scientists know of over a million insect species, but there are probably millions more that no one has discovered yet.

This diagram shows how scientists divide arthropods into smaller groups.

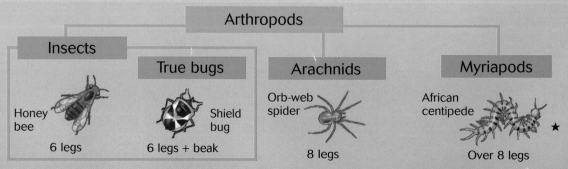

Arthropods

Insects

True bugs

Arachnids

Myriapods

Honey bee
6 legs

Shield bug
6 legs + beak

Orb-web spider
8 legs

African centipede
Over 8 legs

Fact: Bugs far outnumber people. For every person alive today, there are probably several billion bugs.

Myriapods

Bugs with lots of legs, such as centipedes and millipedes, are called myriapods. Centipede means "100 feet" and millipede means "1,000 feet". In fact, some centipedes may have over 300 legs, while some millipedes have as few as 80.

As well as many pairs of legs, this centipede has a pair of poisonous claws, and a pair of feelers on its head.

True bugs

Scientists use the word "bugs" to mean a particular group of insects, also known as true bugs. Like other insects, true bugs have six legs. Unlike other insects, however, they have beaks, which they use to feed. Some true bugs, such as aphids, feed on plants. Others, such as assassin bugs, feed on animals.

Internet links

For links to websites where you can find clickable bug facts and fun online activities, go to **www.usborne-quicklinks.com**

Arachnids

Bugs with eight legs, such as spiders, are called arachnids. Scorpions and mites are also arachnids. Arachnids can be deadly – a few spiders and scorpions can kill people by biting or stinging.

This garden spider is using its eight legs to help it spin a web to catch other bugs for food.

Bug bodies

Bugs' bodies vary enormously in size. Tiny mites are too small to see without a microscope, while some stick insects can be nearly as long as your arm. All bugs' bodies, however, have some features in common.

Internet links

For links to websites where you can see amazing close-up images of bugs' bodies and build your own bugs online, go to **www.usborne-quicklinks.com**

Body parts

Most bugs' bodies are made up of three main parts: a head, a thorax and an abdomen. The head is where the bug's eyes and mouth are, the thorax supports its legs and wings, and the abdomen is where it breaks down its food. In some bugs, such as spiders, the head and thorax are joined together, forming a cephalothorax.

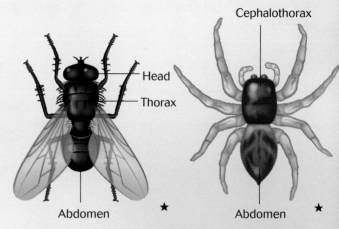

Head

Thorax

Abdomen ★

A fly has three main body parts.

Cephalothorax

Abdomen ★

A spider has two main body parts.

These two wasps are sitting on a cake. Notice their very narrow waists between their thoraxes and abdomens.

Tough bugs

All bugs have a tough outer covering on their bodies. The covering protects their body parts. It is made of a material called chitin, which is hard but light. Bugs don't have bones. This protective covering supports their bodies. It is called an external (outer) skeleton, or exoskeleton.

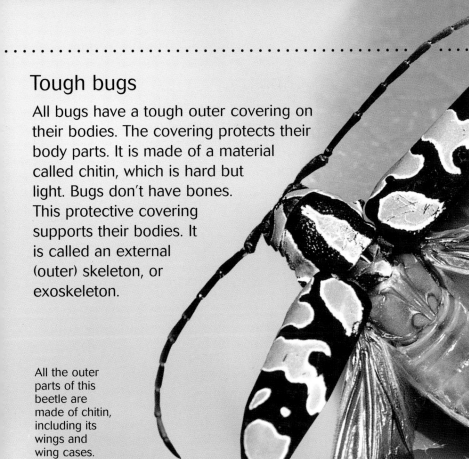

Wing cases

All the outer parts of this beetle are made of chitin, including its wings and wing cases.

Getting bigger

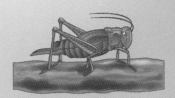

A young cricket grows inside its exoskeleton until it gets too big. Then its exoskeleton starts to split.

The cricket struggles out of its old exoskeleton. Underneath, it has already grown a new one.

The new exoskeleton is soft at first, but it gradually hardens in the air.

Although bugs get bigger, their exoskeletons can't grow. This means that when a bug gets too big, its exoskeleton has to be replaced completely. The bug develops a new, larger exoskeleton and sheds its old one. A bug may shed its exoskeleton several times before it is fully grown.

Fact: Bugs can't get as big as people because an exoskeleton could not support an animal that size. A person-sized bug would collapse under its own weight.

Senses

ike people, bugs can see, hear, feel, taste and smell what is around them. However, bug senses are quite different from people's senses in some ways — for instance, crickets have ears in their knees and flies taste through their feet.

Internet links

For links to websites where you can see what a honeybee sees and find out about bug senses, go to www.usborne-quicklinks.com

Bug-eyed

Most bugs have big eyes, called compound eyes, made up of small units called ommatidia. The ommatidia form separate, overlapping images, like a kaleidoscope. Compound eyes are not good at seeing details clearly, but are great at detecting movement. In addition, some bugs have extra eyes, called simple eyes, which can sense light and dark.

Antennae alert

A bug's feelers, or antennae, are covered in tiny sensitive hairs and bumps. These pick up smells in the air, alerting the bug to food or other bugs. The antennae are also sensitive to touch and can detect movements in the air, helping the bug to feel what is around it.

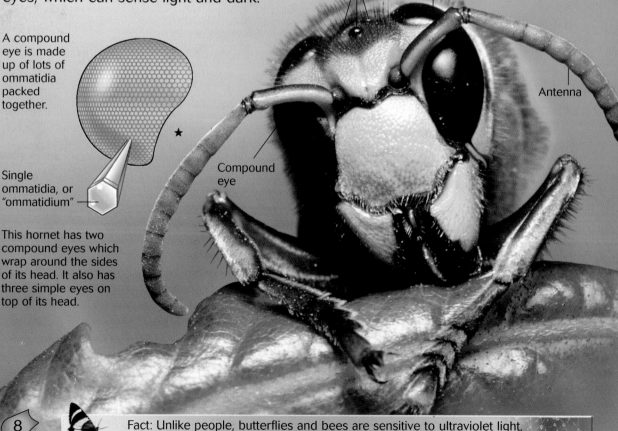

A compound eye is made up of lots of ommatidia packed together.

Single ommatidia, or "ommatidium"

This hornet has two compound eyes which wrap around the sides of its head. It also has three simple eyes on top of its head.

Simple eyes

Compound eye

Antenna

Compound eye

Fact: Unlike people, butterflies and bees are sensitive to ultraviolet light, so they can see markings on flowers that are invisible to us.

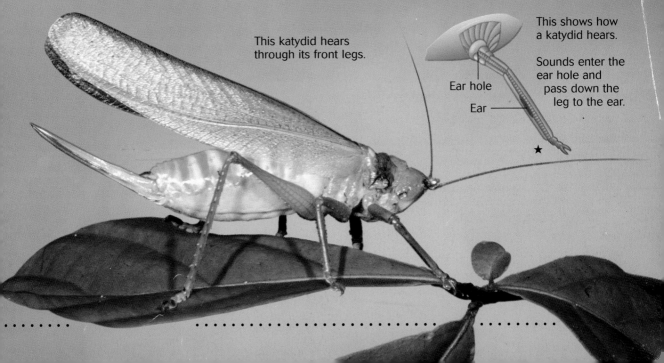

Hairy senses

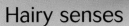

Despite their hard exoskeletons, bugs have a good sense of touch. They have sensitive hairs growing out of their exoskeletons. Bugs can feel when something touches their hairs.

Bugs also have tiny hairs around their mouths which they use to taste things. Some bugs have the same kind of hairs on their feet. This is how flies and butterflies know when they have landed on something good to eat.

This butterfly can tell what kind of plant it has landed on by tasting the leaves with its feet.

Hearing

Bugs can hear a much wider range of sounds than people. Most bugs have ears on their bodies or legs, not on their heads. For example, lacewings have ears in their wings and katydids have ears in their legs. Some bugs also sense noises with their feet – their feet feel movements in the ground caused by noise.

This katydid hears through its front legs.

This shows how a katydid hears.

Sounds enter the ear hole and pass down the leg to the ear.

Ear hole

Ear

On the move ....

Bugs on the move can show amazing strength and speed. For their size, certain bugs can actually run faster and jump higher than people. Flying bugs are also incredible – weight for weight, they can be as powerful as aircraft engines.

High jumps

A few bugs are good at jumping. Grasshoppers and fleas have extra-long hind legs, which they use to push themselves into the air. Cat fleas can jump 17 times their own height. To match that, a person would have to jump about as high as a building with nine floors.

Speedy sprinters

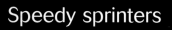

To jump, a grasshopper first bends its hind legs.

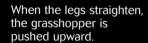

★

When the legs straighten, the grasshopper is pushed upward.

This tiger beetle's long legs make it a very fast runner, helping it to chase and catch its food.

Some bugs, such as sun spiders and house centipedes, have very long legs, which enable them to run fast. The fastest runners are long-legged tiger beetles, which can reach speeds of 9kph (6mph). If an Olympic sprinter and a tiger beetle were the same size, the beetle would easily win a race between them.

.....

On the wing

Many bugs can fly. These bugs have one or two pairs of wings. When a bug flies, muscles in its thorax pull its wings up and down, pushing it up into the air. Flies are some of the fastest fliers – a horsefly has been recorded flying at 145kph (90mph), which is faster than cars usually travel.

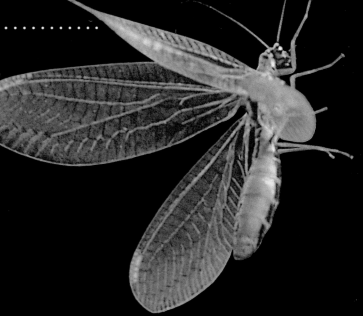

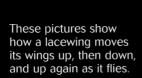

These pictures show how a lacewing moves its wings up, then down, and up again as it flies.

Migrating monarchs

Butterflies have very delicate wings, but they can fly huge distances. Each year, monarch butterflies travel, or migrate, across America, in order to escape harsh winter weather. They fly for days, or even weeks, stopping to rest at night. Some fly more than 3,200km (2,000 miles).

United States of America

Mexico

Key

Where monarchs live in summer

Where monarchs spend the winter

This map shows the journeys made by monarch butterflies to reach their winter resting places.

Internet links

For links to websites with photos and video clips of monarchs, and more about how bugs move, go to **www.usborne-quicklinks.com**

Fact: Flies beat their wings faster than bats or birds – some tiny flies called midges beat their wings up to 1,000 times a second.

Bugs and plants

Bugs and plants need each other to survive. Many bugs eat or live on plants, while most flowering plants depend on bugs to help them to make their seeds.

Caterpillars will hang upside down to eat leaves.

Eating plants

Different plant-eating bugs have different mouths, which are suited to the kinds of plants they eat. For example, caterpillars have jaws that are good for munching leaves, while honey bees have long tongues to drink nectar, a sweet liquid found in flowers. Termites have such strong jaws, they can chew through solid wood.

These leaves are being eaten from the inside by a leaf-miner fly.

The white trails are the tunnels made by the fly as it eats.

Pests and protectors

Certain bugs damage the plants they eat. These bugs are called pests. Some plants are protected by thorns, bristles or a waxy coating, which make them difficult to eat. Other plants have smells or tastes pests don't like. Some bugs help to protect plants by eating pests. For example, young lacewings eat aphids which feed on plant juices.

A young lacewing seizing an aphid in its strong, curved jaws. Young lacewings are so good at catching aphids, they are nicknamed "aphid lions".

Home, sweet home

Many bugs live on or around, or even inside, plants. Young gall wasps and borer beetles live and feed inside trees. The trees grow bumps, called galls, around the bugs. Scientists aren't sure what galls are for, but they may help to stop the bugs from spreading.

Internet links

For links to websites where you can go on a bug hunt in a garden, and search for bugs under a rotting log, go to **www.usborne-quicklinks.com**

Oak tree galls like these are called oak apples.

Gall cut away to show young gall wasp inside.

★

Flower power

Most flowers have markings and smells which attract bugs. They also make a sweet liquid, called nectar, and a powder, called pollen. Bugs visit flowers to drink nectar. At the same time, they pick up pollen and spread it to other flowers. When a flower receives pollen from another flower of the same kind, it can start to make seeds. The seeds will later grow into new flowers.

A bee pushes into a flower to drink nectar. Pollen rubs onto its body.

★ The bee visits a new flower, which picks up some of the pollen.

The yellow dust on this bee is pollen.

Fact: Some plants have flowers which look and smell like rotting meat in order to attract bugs. These plants are called carrion flowers.

Hunting for food

Many bugs hunt small animals, often other bugs, for food. They have different ways of catching their prey (the animals they eat). Some rely on speed, while others set traps for their unlucky victims.

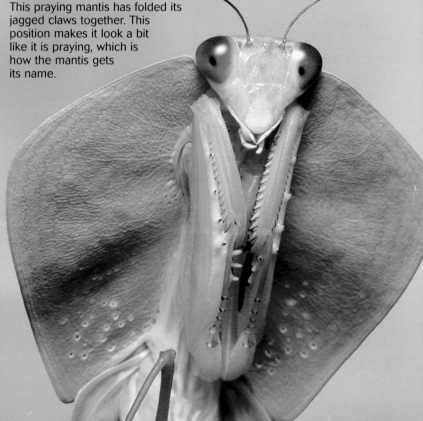

This beetle is such a fierce hunter, it is known as a tiger beetle.

Claws

Some bugs have sharp claws to help them catch their prey. Praying mantids have claws with jagged edges, to help grip their prey and stop it from slipping away. Centipedes have poisonous claws, which they use to stab and poison small animals.

Fast movers

Bugs that move quickly can catch their prey by chasing it. Wolf spiders and long-legged tiger beetles can run fast, chasing bugs on the ground. Dragonflies and robber flies chase bugs in the air. These flies are so quick, they can even catch fast-flying mosquitoes.

This praying mantis has folded its jagged claws together. This position makes it look a bit like it is praying, which is how the mantis gets its name.

A praying mantis stays very still as it waits for its prey to come within reach of its claws.

When the prey is close enough, the mantis strikes, seizing it in a twentieth of a second.

Trap door

Trap-door spiders make burrows in the ground to catch their prey. The entrance to a burrow is hidden by a trap door made of silk and mud. The spider waits behind the door. When an insect walks past, the spider darts out and catches it.

This is a trap-door spider. These spiders use their fangs to dig burrows.

Smelly beetle

One kind of beetle looks like a piece of dung, and can even make itself smell like dung. It sits very still and waits for the smell to attract a fly. When a fly lands, the beetle leaps on it and eats it.

Internet links

For links to websites where you can watch videos of bugs eating their prey, with photos and facts, go to **www.usborne-quicklinks.com**

Antlion pit

Antlions are a kind of baby insect. They trap ants and other small insects by digging pits in sandy soil. Then they hide in the sand at the bottom of the pit, with only their large, toothed jaws showing, and wait for their prey.

An ant falls into an antlion pit and slides down the side.

The antlion flicks sand at the ant, to make it slide faster.

At the bottom, the antlion seizes the ant and eats it.

In disguise ....

Some bugs have developed clever disguises to help them catch prey or avoid being caught. Most bugs use their disguises to hide, but some bugs disguise themselves by copying the eye-catching markings of poisonous bugs.

This leaf katydid has large wings that look just like leaves.

Hide-and-seek

Bugs that blend in with their background are less likely to be seen and eaten by other animals. For example, green grasshoppers are safest from birds when they are hidden among green grasses.

★

On a white and green leaf, a crab spider will be white and green.

When the spider moves to a yellow flower, it turns yellow.

Bugs that hunt can catch their prey more easily if they blend in. Crab spiders hide on plants to catch other bugs. The spiders can change their looks to match the plant where they are lying in wait.

Complete disguise

Some bugs don't just blend in, but are completely disguised as something else. Stick insects look like twigs, and leaf katydids are green and leaf-shaped. Pink orchid mantids have pink bodies and petal-shaped legs, making them look like pink orchid flowers.

The strange appearance of this pink orchid mantis fools insects into landing on it to look for nectar.

Warning markings

Poisonous bugs often have warning markings in orange or yellow and black. Most animals have learned to avoid eating bugs with these markings. Wasps and bees, which can sting, have black and yellow stripes. Orange and black monarch butterflies taste awful and, if eaten, usually make animals sick.

This is a monarch butterfly. Monarch butterflies are poisonous because they grow up feeding on milkweed, which makes most animals sick.

Wasps like this one have painful stings which they can use again and again.

Copycats

Some harmless bugs have the same markings as poisonous bugs. This is called mimicry. Although these bugs might be good to eat, most animals are put off by their copycat disguises. Hover flies can't sting, but are striped like wasps. Viceroy butterflies are harmless, but look like monarch butterflies.

This viceroy butterfly looks very like a monarch butterfly, apart from the extra black stripe you can see on its wings.

As well as looking like a wasp, this hover fly can buzz like a wasp.

Internet links

For links to websites where you can build a caterpillar and find out more about insect mimicry, go to **www.usborne-quicklinks.com**

Fact: Elephant hawk moth caterpillars disguise themselves as snakes. If frightened, they puff themselves up and display markings that look like a snake's eyes.

Finding a mate

M ost bugs have to find a mate (a bug
of the opposite sex) before they
can produce baby bugs. Different bugs
have different ways of attracting a mate.
Some dance or make noises, while
others create light displays
or smells.

The male
spider attracts
the female by
plucking on
her web with
his legs.

Most female spiders
are much larger
than their mates.

Attention seekers

Male spiders have various ways of
attracting a female's attention. Some
dance or drum their legs on the ground.
Others look for female spiders' webs.
When a male finds a web, he plucks on
it in a particular rhythm. This plucking
lets the female know that a possible
mate is nearby.

Big noises

Male grasshoppers, crickets and cicadas
attract females by "singing". Grasshoppers
and crickets make chirping noises by
rubbing parts of their bodies together.
Cicadas have a layer of chitin, called a
tymbal, in their abdomens. They click
their tymbals back and forth very fast,
making a loud buzzing noise.

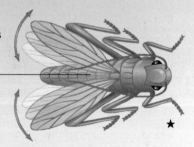

Crickets sing by
moving their wings
back and forth.

Rough parts on
the wings rub
against each other
to make a noise.

Internet links

For links to websites where you can help a male
spider pluck a web and watch a courtship dance
video, go to **www.usborne-quicklinks.com**

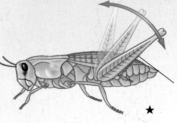

Grasshoppers sing
by moving their legs
up and down.

Bumps on the legs rub
against ridges on the
wings to make a noise.

Fact: Some kinds of cicadas can make more noise than a chainsaw.

Smelly moths

Female moths attract mates by making smells called pheromones. Male moths have big, feathery feelers which can detect pheromones from a great distance. Each kind of moth has a different smell, so that the males can find the right females.

With its huge feelers, this male emperor moth can smell a female 10km (6 miles) away.

Bright lights

During the day, fireflies look like ordinary beetles.

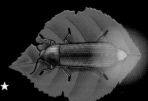

At night, fireflies produce a bright light.

★

Glow-worms and fireflies are beetles that can make their own light. Chemicals in the beetles' abdomens produce red, green or orange light. Male and female beetles use flashes of light to signal to each other.

The mating game

Finding a mate can be a dangerous business. Female spiders and praying mantids will occasionally eat their mates. Some male spiders try to avoid this by giving their partners dead insects to eat instead.

This male spider is offering his partner a dead insect to eat, wrapped up in spider silk.

Baby bugs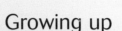

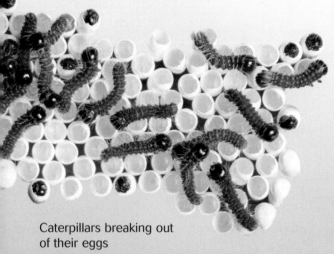

Baby bugs usually start out in eggs. Parent bugs lay eggs in all sorts of places – on plants, in the ground, or even inside other animals – but nearly always somewhere where there will be food for their babies.

Caterpillars breaking out of their eggs

Hatching and after

Bugs' eggs have strong eggshells, made of chitin, which protect the babies inside as they develop. When the babies are big enough, they break out of their eggs, or hatch.

Outside the eggs, the babies continue to develop and start to look for food. Most have to find food and avoid enemies by themselves, as only a few bug parents look after their babies.

Unusually for bugs, tortoise beetles are good parents. This tortoise beetle mother is guarding her eggs from bugs which might eat them.

Growing up

Some baby bugs, such as baby silverfish and spiders, look exactly like tiny adults. The babies get bigger and bigger as they grow up, shedding their exoskeletons from time to time, until they are fully grown.

Internet links

For links to websites where you can take an interactive look at baby bugs, go to **www.usborne-quicklinks.com**

Changing shape

Bugs that can fly have babies that don't look exactly like the adults. These bugs actually start out without wings. As they grow up, their shapes change and they develop wings. This is called metamorphosis, and there are two ways it can happen.

A mother cockroach and her babies. The mother has wings under her wing cases, but the babies don't and can't yet fly.

Budding wings

Baby cockroaches and grasshoppers look like small adults with no wings. Baby bugs like this are called nymphs. As the nymphs grow, they develop wing buds. Each time they shed their exoskeletons, their wing buds get bigger, until they have full-sized wings.

This diagram shows the stages a grasshopper goes through as it grows up.

1. An adult grasshopper lays lots of eggs.

2. A wingless nymph hatches out of each egg.

4. The grasshopper develops wings as it grows.

3. The nymph grows and sheds its exoskeleton.

Body changes

Baby beetles, butterflies and bees look very different from adults. Baby bugs like this are called larvae. The larvae grow for a few weeks, then turn into pupae. From outside, the pupae look lifeless. Inside, however, the bugs are becoming winged adults.

This diagram shows the stages a ladybird beetle (ladybug) goes through as it grows up.

1. An adult beetle lays lots of eggs.

2. A wingless larva hatches out of each egg.

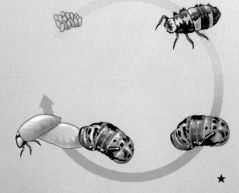

4. The beetle emerges as a fully-grown adult.

3. The larva grows, then turns into a pupa.

Fact: It takes less than a week for a baby aphid to grow up and have babies of its own.

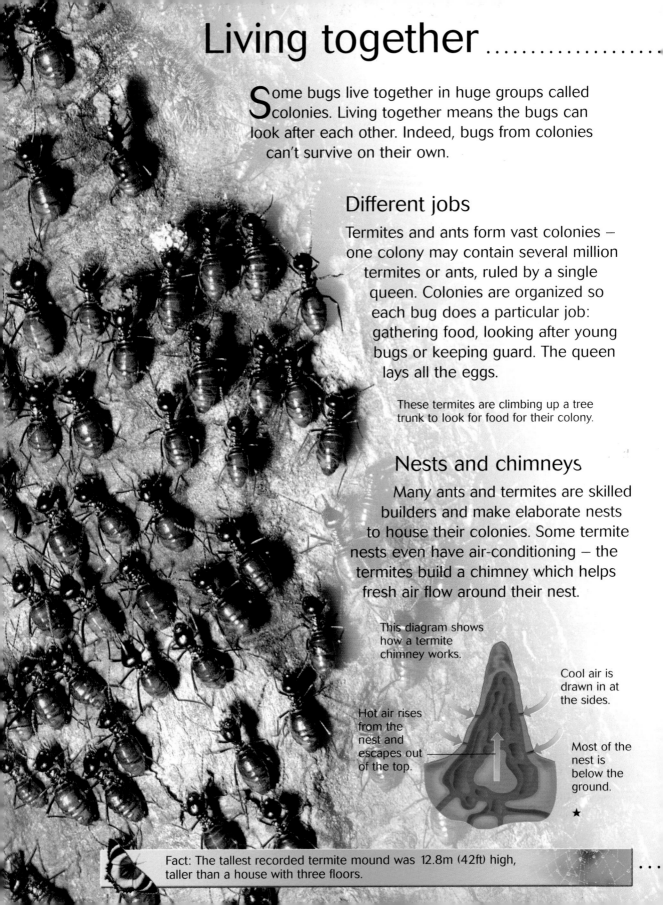

Living together ....

Some bugs live together in huge groups called colonies. Living together means the bugs can look after each other. Indeed, bugs from colonies can't survive on their own.

Different jobs

Termites and ants form vast colonies – one colony may contain several million termites or ants, ruled by a single queen. Colonies are organized so each bug does a particular job: gathering food, looking after young bugs or keeping guard. The queen lays all the eggs.

These termites are climbing up a tree trunk to look for food for their colony.

Nests and chimneys

Many ants and termites are skilled builders and make elaborate nests to house their colonies. Some termite nests even have air-conditioning – the termites build a chimney which helps fresh air flow around their nest.

This diagram shows how a termite chimney works.

Cool air is drawn in at the sides.

Hot air rises from the nest and escapes out of the top.

Most of the nest is below the ground.

★

Fact: The tallest recorded termite mound was 12.8m (42ft) high, taller than a house with three floors.

Inside a honey-bee nest

The walls of the cells are made of wax.

These cells hold honey (concentrated nectar). They have been sealed with wax.

This worker bee is sealing a cell.

These cells are full of pollen.

These cells are being filled with honey.

Busy bees

Honey bees live in some of the most highly-organized colonies. Each colony is made up of female workers, ruled by a queen who lays all the eggs. The workers build and defend the nest, look after larvae, gather food and make honey. Once a year, male drones are born. The drones mate with the queen, then die.

Internet links

For links to websites where you can explore an interactive beehive, watch video clips of bee dances and play a termite game, go to **www.usborne-quicklinks.com**

Dancing bees

When a worker bee returns to the nest from gathering food, it will dance in front of the other bees, moving around in circles and waggling its body. The dance shows the other bees how far away the food is, and in what direction, so they can find it too.

This diagram shows the "round dance", where a bee moves in a circle, first one way, then the other. This shows it has found food within 80m (260ft) of the nest.

In the ground

Many different kinds of bugs live in the ground. Some live underground for just part of their lives, while others never leave the ground at all. Although well-hidden, underground bugs can have very visible effects, especially on plants.

Hidey-holes

A hole in the ground is a good hiding place for young bugs. There, they are protected from the weather and from animals which might eat them. Earwigs grow up in underground nests, where their mothers bring them food. Many caterpillars and beetles grow up underground too.

This earwig mother will look after her babies underground until they grow up.

Underground attack

Some bug pests damage plants by attacking them underground. For example, wireworms (young click beetles) and leatherjackets (crane fly larvae) feed on plants' roots. Cutworms (moth caterpillars) can be especially destructive because they eat all the way through plants' stems.

★

A cutworm feeds at night, chewing through plants' stems just below the ground's surface.

By day, the cutworm hides underground. The plants with cut stems wither and die.

Internet links

For links to websites where you can go on an underground bug adventure and find out about cicadas that grow up underground, go to **www.usborne-quicklinks.com**

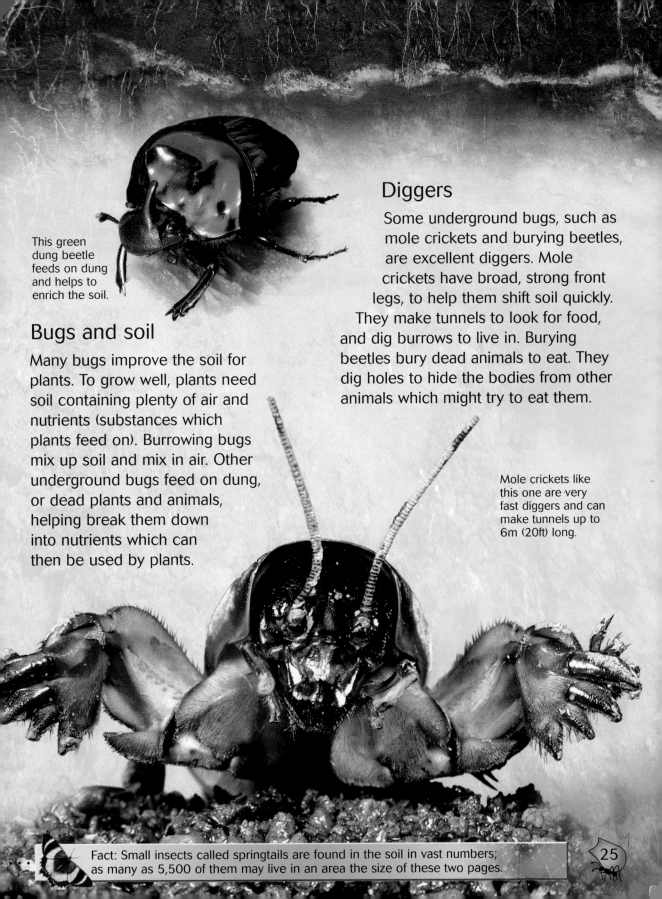

This green dung beetle feeds on dung and helps to enrich the soil.

Diggers

Some underground bugs, such as mole crickets and burying beetles, are excellent diggers. Mole crickets have broad, strong front legs, to help them shift soil quickly. They make tunnels to look for food, and dig burrows to live in. Burying beetles bury dead animals to eat. They dig holes to hide the bodies from other animals which might try to eat them.

Bugs and soil

Many bugs improve the soil for plants. To grow well, plants need soil containing plenty of air and nutrients (substances which plants feed on). Burrowing bugs mix up soil and mix in air. Other underground bugs feed on dung, or dead plants and animals, helping break them down into nutrients which can then be used by plants.

Mole crickets like this one are very fast diggers and can make tunnels up to 6m (20ft) long.

Fact: Small insects called springtails are found in the soil in vast numbers; as many as 5,500 of them may live in an area the size of these two pages.

Underwater...

M any bugs live in and around
water – in streams, ponds, rivers
and lakes. However, very few bugs
live in the seas or oceans. Some
bugs that live in water are
very good swimmers, but
not all of them can breathe
underwater.

The dips in the water surface
around this pond skater's feet are
caused by water-repelling hairs.

Swimming

Great diving
beetles and water
boatmen are excellent
swimmers and divers.
They can store bubbles of
air, which they use to breathe
while underwater. Diving beetles
keep air under their wings, while
water boatmen trap air under their
bodies. To breathe, the bugs take in
the stored air through holes in their
exoskeletons called spiracles.

This water boatman is using
its long, oar-like legs to push
itself through the water.

On the surface

Pond skaters and whirligig
beetles live on the water
surface, eating insects
which fall in. Pond skaters
walk on the water – they
have long legs which
spread out their weight,
so they don't sink.
Whirligig beetles swim
around in circles
looking for their prey.

This diving beetle has
caught a small fish to eat.
Diving beetles also eat
snails and tadpoles.

Internet links

For links to websites where you can
discover different water bugs, go to
www.usborne-quicklinks.com

Fact: Whirligig beetles have four eyes, enabling them to see above
and below the water at the same time.

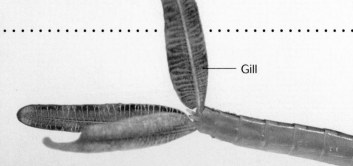

— Gill

This is a damselfly nymph. It breathes through gills at the end of its abdomen. It will live underwater until it becomes a winged adult.

Water babies

Several kinds of bugs grow up underwater, including dragonflies, damselflies and mayflies. The young bugs have feathery structures, called gills, which allow them to breathe underwater like fish. However, the adults can only breathe air and live on land.

Underwater webs

Water spiders live underwater, but need air to breathe. They make underwater air bubbles to live in, swimming out to catch passing water insects for food.

A water spider makes a dome-shaped web attached to water weeds.

The spider swims to the surface and traps a bubble of air with its legs.

The spider returns to its web and releases the bubble, filling the web with air.

At the bottom

Young caddisflies and drone flies live at the bottom of ponds and streams. Drone fly larvae live in the mud and breathe through long tubes, which look like tails. Caddisfly larvae live inside protective cases, which they make themselves out of bits of shells, stones or leaves.

See how this caddisfly larva is covered in a case of tiny stones.

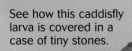

True bugs

True bugs are a particular group of bugs. They are insects with beaks. They use their beaks to pierce the skin of their food. Some true bugs feed on plant juices, while others attack animals to drink their blood or body fluids.

Bugs with beaks

Beak

When unfolded, a true bug's beak sticks out like this, ready to stab its food.

Folded beak

★

When not eating, the bug can fold its beak up out of the way.

A true bug's beak (sometimes called a rostrum) sticks out from its head. The bug's mouth is inside the beak. To feed, the bug pushes its beak into its food and uses it like a drinking straw, sucking liquid through it.

Internet links

For links to websites where you can play online quiz games about bugs that live on humans, go to **www.usborne-quicklinks.com**

This adult periodical cicada is resting with its beak tucked away under its body.

Long lives

Periodical cicadas are true bugs with long lives and an unusual life-cycle. Young cicadas spend years underground, sucking juices from tree roots – one kind stays underground for 17 years. Then all the cicadas emerge at once, mate and lay eggs. When the eggs hatch, the young cicadas burrow back underground to live until they are ready to mate.

Fact: One kind of true bug is called the kissing bug because it sometimes bites people's faces.

Assassins

Assassin bugs hunt other bugs. When they catch one, they use their beaks to stab it and inject it with a poison that dissolves its insides. They then suck up the dissolved insides, leaving behind a hollow skin or shell.

This assassin bug has caught a plump caterpillar to eat.

Blood-suckers

Bed bugs are small, orangey-brown bugs that feed on human blood. They hide in bedding or in cracks in walls. At night, they come out to eat. They can drink up to five times their own weight in blood.

★

This bed bug has been drawn six times life-size.

Stink bugs

Shield bugs have bright, shield-shaped bodies. They feed on plants and other bugs. They are nicknamed stink bugs because they give off a bad smell when they are frightened.

This shield bug has sucked its prey dry, leaving only a shrivelled skin.

Beetles

There are more beetles than any other kind of bug. About a quarter of all known animal species are beetles. They live in all sorts of places, including water, wood and soil. Some beetles, such as carpet beetles and biscuit beetles, like to live in people's houses.

This bright, spotted beetle lives and feeds on plants. It is called a spotted cucumber beetle.

Built like tanks

Beetles are insects. They have strong jaws and tough exoskeletons. In fact, they are built a bit like tanks, so they can burrow under stones or crawl through soil without being crushed. Some beetles even tunnel through solid wood.

Flying

All beetles have wings and most beetles can fly. When they are not flying, their wings are protected by hard wing cases. The wing cases meet in a straight line down the middle of their backs.

At rest, a beetle's wing cases completely cover its wings.

★

To fly, the beetle holds the wing cases sideways, out of the way of its wings.

Pests

A few beetles can be great pests. Some beetles, such as the Colorado potato beetle, damage and destroy farm crops. Others, such as deathwatch beetles, invade and damage people's houses.

Fact: Goliath beetles are the heaviest insects. A large goliath beetle can weigh as much as 100g (3.5oz), which is about the same as an apple.

This ladybird beetle (ladybug) is about to devour an aphid. One beetle may eat 5,000 aphids in its life.

Internet links

For links to websites with online learning games about beetles and ladybirds, go to **www.usborne-quicklinks.com**

Beetle wrestling

Stag beetles live on tree branches. Male stag beetles have huge jaws that look like antlers. If one male stag beetle invades another's branch, the two of them will wrestle. Each beetle tries to grab the other in his jaws. A beetle wins by seizing his opponent and flipping him over onto his back. The winner gets to stay on the branch.

Helpful beetles

Many beetles are useful to people. Aphids damage garden plants, but ladybird beetles (or ladybugs) help protect plants by eating aphids. Other beetles help to clean up waste. For example, dung beetles clean up dung by eating it, and by collecting balls of dung for their young to eat.

This stag beetle is about to throw his opponent off his branch.

See how this dung beetle is using its back legs to roll a ball of dung. When the ball is finished, the beetle will bury it.

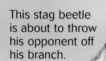

Butterflies and moths

Butterflies and moths are closely related insects, and all have two pairs of wings. Butterflies' wings are covered in tiny scales which create bright, shimmering patterns. Moths' wings usually have patterns that are less bright.

Bright and beautiful

The bright markings on a butterfly's wings help other butterflies to recognize it. Some markings look like eyes. These "eyes" can startle attackers and fool them into leaving the butterflies alone.

The blue "eye" spots on this butterfly's wings help to frighten away birds which might attack it.

With their wings open, most butterflies display eye-catching patterns.

With their wings shut, the markings are covered and the butterflies can hide.

Night fliers

Moths usually fly around at night, although you sometimes see them during the day. There are many more species of moths than butterflies. The best way to tell moths and butterflies apart is to look at their antennae (feelers). Butterfly antennae have knobs at the end, while moth antennae tend to be feathery.

Feathery antennae

This atlas moth is resting with its wings spread out. Atlas moths have the largest wings of any moth, measuring up to 30cm (1ft) from wingtip to wingtip.

Fact: Once they become adults, most butterflies live for only a few days or weeks, although some kinds can survive for several months.

Starting out

Butterflies and moths start out in eggs. Inside each egg is a tiny caterpillar. The caterpillar hatches and starts to eat and grow, shedding its skin from time to time. When it is big enough, it makes a protective case around itself. At this stage of its life, it is called a pupa. Inside the case, its body changes. Eventually, it emerges as an adult butterfly or moth.

This diagram shows a butterfly's life cycle.

1. An adult butterfly lays several eggs.

2. A caterpillar hatches out of each egg.

4. An adult butterfly emerges from the case.

3. Each caterpillar makes a case around itself.

Flower food

Most butterflies and moths feed on the sugary nectar produced by flowers. Nectar is found deep inside flowers. To reach it, butterflies and moths have a long tube, called a proboscis, that they use like a drinking straw. When they are not feeding, they coil up the proboscis to keep it out of the way.

This swallowtail butterfly is using its long proboscis to drink nectar from a flower.

Internet links

For links to websites where you can watch butterfly videos, print out and shade in pictures of a butterfly's life cycle and solve puzzles, go to **www.usborne-quicklinks.com**

Flies

M any kinds of insects are called "flies". Some, such as large dragonflies and tiny mayflies, have two pairs of wings. Others, known as true flies, only have one pair of wings. True flies include horse flies, house flies and mosquitoes.

A house fly like this carries around two and a half million germs in and on its body.

Fast flyers

As their name suggests, most flies are good at flying, with wings powered by strong flight muscles inside their thorax. Dragonflies and horse flies are especially fast fliers: an emperor dragonfly can reach almost 100kph (60mph), while a horse fly may reach 145kph (90mph).

Robber flies are powerful fliers and hunt in the air. This one has caught a shorter fly and landed to eat it.

Flying stunts

Instead of a second pair of wings, true flies have a pair of stick-like growths called halteres. Halteres help true flies to balance, so they can perform amazing flying stunts. They can hover in the same place, turn on the spot or even fly backwards and upside down.

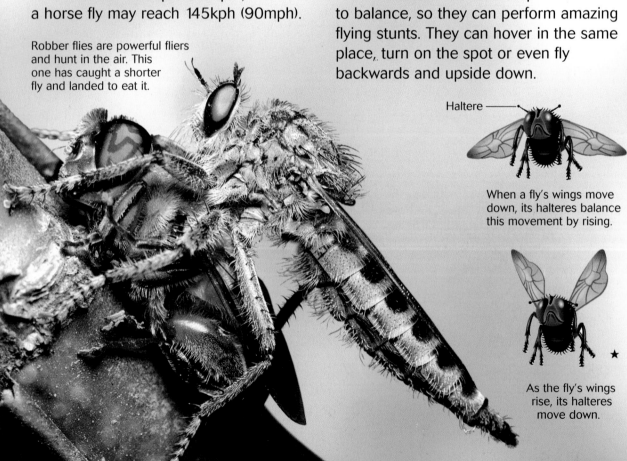

Haltere

When a fly's wings move down, its halteres balance this movement by rising.

As the fly's wings rise, its halteres move down.

Horrible habits

When a fly lands on food, it covers the food in spit.

The fly's spit turns the food into a soupy liquid.

The fly then slurps up the liquid, using spongy pads on its mouth to mop it up.

★

House flies and bluebottles like to eat all sorts of things, including dung and rotting meat. These flies can taste through their feet, which are covered in sensitive hairs. This is how they know they have landed on something to eat.

Blood suckers

Some flies feed on blood. These flies have sharp jaws which can pierce skin. They drink blood from many kinds of animals. Some mosquitoes like to feed on people's blood. When a mosquito bites, it injects you with saliva to make your blood easier to drink. Your skin reacts to the saliva, causing an itchy bite.

Internet links

For links to websites on dragonflies and other types of flies, with a fun online game to play, go to **www.usborne-quicklinks.com**

Helpful flies

Although flies can be a nuisance, we could not live without them. Some flies spread pollen, which helps plants to make seeds. Other flies eat harmful bugs, keeping down their numbers. Flies are also a source of food for insect-eating animals.

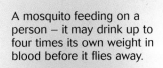

A mosquito feeding on a person – it may drink up to four times its own weight in blood before it flies away.

Fact: Not all flies can fly. Some, such as sheep ked flies and bee louse flies, don't even have wings.

35

Ants, bees and wasps......................

Although ants can look very different from bees and wasps, they are fairly closely related to them. Ants, bees and wasps all belong to the same group of insects, and they have many features in common.

Wasp waists

Ants, bees and wasps have a very narrow waist (sometimes called a "wasp waist") between their thorax and abdomen.

These diagrams show the similarities between an ant, a wasp and a bee.

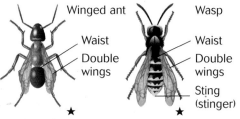

Winged ant
Waist
Double wings

Wasp
Waist
Double wings
Sting (stinger)

Bee
Waist
Double wings
Sting (stinger)

This is a bumble bee. Its fuzzy hairs help it to collect pollen, which sticks to the hairs when it visits a flower.

A sting in the tail

Wasps, bees and some ants have sharp stings (or "stingers") they can use to inject enemies or prey with poison. A wasp can sting again and again, but a bee can only sting once. When a bee stings someone, it leaves its sting behind. This damages its insides and it soon dies.

Hooked wings

Bees, wasps and winged ants have two pairs of wings: a big front pair and a small back pair. The back wings are attached to the front wings by a row of tiny hooks, so the wings move together. Scientists think that this helps these bugs fly more efficiently.

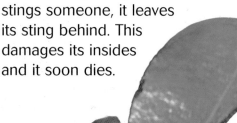

Making a home

Some bees and wasps build elaborate homes. Honey bees build large shared nests out of wax, and paper wasps make shared nests from a papery mush of chewed-up wood. However, most bees and wasps live on their own and make individual nests. Some dig holes in the ground, while others build tiny pot-shaped nests out of mud.

Organized ants

All ants live together in big groups called colonies. Within each colony, different ants do different jobs: soldiers guard the colony, workers find food and the queen lays eggs. Slave-maker ant colonies are unusual because they don't have their own workers. Instead, they capture and raise young ants from other colonies to do their work for them.

This is a paper wasps' nest. As you can see, these wasps make round, hanging nests, with the entrance at the bottom.

These are leafcutter ant workers. Leafcutter ants feed on fungus, which they grow on cut leaves. The ants here are gathering leaves for their colony.

Internet links

For links to sites where you can watch leafcutter ants on a webcam and explore a bee's anatomy, go to **www.usborne-quicklinks.com**

Fact: Some wasps lay their eggs inside other animals, such as caterpillars. When the eggs hatch, the young wasps eat the animal from the inside.

Spiders

All spiders have eight legs, but different spiders can vary a lot in size. They can be smaller than ants or as big as dinner plates. The biggest spider in the world is the giant bird-eating spider, from South America, which can be up to 28cm (11in) across.

Hunters

Spiders hunt other animals to eat. To hunt, they need good senses. Although most spiders have eight eyes, many can't see well. However, all spiders are covered in sensitive hairs. These hairs can feel the spiders' surroundings and pick up smells, helping them to find and catch their prey.

Poison fangs

Spiders have poison fangs. They can kill a smaller animal, or leave it unable to move, by biting it with their fangs. Few spiders are dangerous to people, but bites from the Brazilian wandering spider and the black widow spider can be deadly if they are not treated.

Black widow spiders like this inject a poison 15 times stronger than rattlesnake poison with each bite.

Internet links

For links to websites where you can explore a spider's body, watch video clips and play a game, go to **www.usborne-quicklinks.com**

This spider is known as a red-kneed tarantula spider because of the stripes on its legs.

The spider's eyes are on top of its head.

Abdomen

Cephalothorax

Sensitive hairs

This spider has made an orb web with a zigzag pattern. A visible pattern helps birds avoid blundering into the web by mistake. It may also help attract insects by imitating patterns on flowers.

Eating habits

Spiders can only eat liquids. When a spider catches another bug, it wraps the bug in silk and injects it with juices which turn its insides into liquid. Then the spider sucks out the liquid, using hairs in its mouth to filter out lumps.

Spider silk

All spiders can make silk. They produce liquid silk in their abdomens, then spin it into threads by squeezing it out of holes in their abdomens called spinnerets. The silk is light, strong and stretchy. Many spiders make silk webs to catch food, but different spiders make differently shaped webs, depending on their prey.

This spider is wrapping its prey in silk to stop it from escaping.

An orb web is strung up in the air, to catch flying insects.

A sheet web is made close to the ground, to catch crawling insects.

Tangle webs are often made in the corners of rooms by house spiders.

Fact: The biggest and strongest spiders' webs are made by golden orb-web spiders. Their webs may be up to 2m (6.5ft) wide and can trap small birds.

Bad bugs

Lots of people don't like bugs, and many bugs spread diseases or destroy crops. These are the bad guys of the bug world.

Deadly diseases

Bugs can pass on diseases when they feed on our blood or our food. Fleas and mosquitoes spread deadly diseases such as typhus and yellow fever. Flies and cockroaches spread germs which cause food poisoning.

In the past, more people died from diseases spread by bugs than from any other cause. Even today, about one-sixth of the world's population suffers from diseases spread by bugs.

Tiny killer

The tiny female anopheles mosquito is one of the deadliest bugs in the world. Its bites spread a disease called malaria. Although malaria can be treated, it still kills about two million people each year.

This diagram explains how malaria spreads.

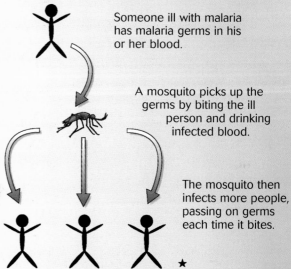

Someone ill with malaria has malaria germs in his or her blood.

A mosquito picks up the germs by biting the ill person and drinking infected blood.

The mosquito then infects more people, passing on germs each time it bites.

Cockroaches invade houses looking for food. These cockroaches are feeding on a cake they have found.

Internet links

For links to websites on destructive pests in homes, with online activities and games, go to **www.usborne-quicklinks.com**

Fact: Only female mosquitoes drink blood, because they need the protein to help them develop their eggs. Male mosquitoes live on plant juices.

This pumpkin leaf has been badly damaged by the grasshoppers feeding on it.

Destroyers

Many bugs cause huge damage to plants, and farm crops are especially at risk. On farms, lots of the same plants are grown together, creating good conditions for pests. Of all the crops grown in the world, about one-fifth are eaten by bugs or affected by the diseases they carry.

Hungry bugs

Locusts (a kind of grasshopper) are plant-eaters with big appetites, devouring their own weight in food each day. Although they are small, they travel and feed in huge groups, or swarms. A swarm may contain tens of millions of locusts, which together eat thousands of tons of food a day, destroying plants and leaving people and animals to starve.

This group of locusts will kill these plants by eating all their leaves.

Helpful bugs......................................

Although some bugs cause damage or spread diseases, there are many helpful bugs too. In fact, we need bugs to survive. Without bugs, the world would be a very different place.

Living world

Bugs are an essential part of the world around us. Helpful bugs spread plant pollen, kill pests, clear away waste and improve the soil. Without them, we would be swamped by pests and dirt, and many plants would be unable to make seeds and would die out. Most fruit and vegetable plants, including apples, oranges and onions, depend on bugs to spread their pollen – without bugs, we would lose about a third of our food.

Bug food

Bugs are an important food for many animals, including fish, frogs, bats, birds and bears. Some people eat bugs too. Over 500 bug species, including termites, grasshoppers and caterpillars, are eaten by people in different parts of the world.

Along with bees, beetles such as this flower beetle play a vital role in spreading pollen between flowers.

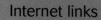

Internet links

For links to websites where you can find out about bugs that are both good and bad, go to **www.usborne-quicklinks.com**

This is a can of mopani worms. These worms (a kind of moth caterpillar) are a popular food in Africa.

Fact: People used to bandage cuts and wounds with spiders' webs. This helped stop infections as spiders' webs contain an antibiotic.

Making silk

Silk moth caterpillars, or silkworms, use their silky spit to form cocoons. Each cocoon consists of a single strand of silk over 1km (half a mile) long. People farm silkworms and use their cocoons to make silk fabric. It takes up to 2,000 cocoons to make enough silk for a dress.

A silk moth laying eggs on a cocoon. Only cocoons that are not used for silk develop into moths.

Silkworms hatch out of silk moth eggs and feed on chopped mulberry leaves.

After a month, each silkworm makes a silky cocoon around itself and becomes a pupa.

The cocoons are boiled to loosen the silk, so it can be wound onto a reel.

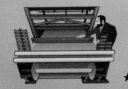

Once the silk is cleaned and spun into thread, it is woven into fabric on a loom.

Honey and seeds

Honey bees collect nectar from flowers to make honey. To make 500g (1lb) of honey, a colony of bees has to visit about two million flowers. The bees also spread pollen between those flowers, helping the plants to make seeds.

This beekeeper is inspecting bees on a farm. His white suit protects him from bee stings.

Medical maggots

Maggots eat rotting meat, but won't eat living flesh. In experiments, they have been used to clean people's wounds. They eat away any dead flesh in the wound, but don't damage healthy flesh. They also give off a natural antibiotic (a substance that helps to stop infections).

Amazing facts ....

Bugs live in all kinds of places, and have developed some surprising characteristics and habits. On these pages, you can discover some of the most amazing bug facts.

The very thick, strong exoskeleton of this rhinoceros beetle helps it to carry huge weights.

🐞 If you weighed all the bugs in the world, they would be heavier than all the other animals put together.

🐞 The weight of bugs eaten each year by spiders is greater than the weight of all the people in the world.

🐞 Tiny bugs called mites have been found in hummingbirds' nostrils, under snakes' scales and inside moths' ears. You probably have harmless mites living on your eyelashes.

🐞 Fairyflies are the smallest insects in the world. They are only 0.02cm (0.008in) long. They are not really flies, but a kind of wasp.

🐞 Female fairyflies lay their eggs inside the eggs of other insects. They insert their eggs using their sting.

🐞 Harvester ants produce the most powerful poison of any insect. The poison is injected when they sting, and it takes only 12 harvester ant stings to kill a rat.

🐞 Rhinoceros beetles are some of the strongest animals in the world. They can carry about 850 times their own weight. That's like a person carrying 75 cars.

🐞 Cockroaches have been found living in all kinds of places, including inside computers, where they can cause short-circuits. This led to the term "computer bug".

🐞 Cockroaches can live for a week without water, and for a month without food. They can even survive for a week without their heads.

This cockroach could survive very harsh conditions, and even losing its head.

When alarmed, the bombardier beetle defends itself by squirting boiling liquid from the tip of its abdomen. The liquid comes out with a pop and a puff of smoke.

When in danger, one kind of South African cockroach stands on its head and hisses.

Some termites will blow themselves up to defend their nests. The exploding termites block the nest's entrances and splatter attackers with their insides.

Cheese skippers are tiny maggots that are sometimes found in cheese. They can "skip" (jump) by bending and straightening their bodies.

Fleas can jump up and down for several days without stopping.

Flies can walk upside down on ceilings because they have sticky pads, like suction cups, at the ends of their feet.

Crushed mealybugs are used to make a red food dye called cochineal.

Woodlice (sowbugs) are more closely related to sea-creatures such as crabs than to insects and other bugs on land.

Scuttle flies seem to eat almost anything, including shoe polish and paint.

Caterpillars spend most of their time eating. Polyphemus moth caterpillars can eat 86,000 times their own weight before they turn into pupae.

Certain species of moths will only feed on tears, while vampire moths drink only blood.

Some moths and butterflies never eat at all. They live on energy stored from the food that they ate while they were caterpillars.

Diopsid flies can see around corners, because their eyes are on stalks.

A firebrat (a kind of insect) may replace its exoskeleton as many as 60 times over the course of its life.

Weevils are beetles with unusually long noses. They use their noses to drill holes in plants, where they lay their eggs.

This weevil's nose is almost as long as its body. Its mouth is at the tip of its nose.

Acknowledgements ....

Every effort has been made to trace the copyright holders of the material in this book. If any rights have been omitted, the publishers offer to rectify this in any subsequent editions following notification. The publishers are grateful to the following organizations and individuals for their permission to reproduce material (t=top, m=middle, b=bottom, l=left, r=right):

Cover © G. Bernard/Oxford Scientific Films; **p1** © Digital Vision; **p2–3** © Digital Vision; **p4** (t) © S. Dalton/Natural History Photographic Agency; **p5** (t) © D. Hosking/Frank Lane Picture Agency; (b) © F. Muntarda/CORBIS; **p6** (b) © A. & H. Michler/Science Photo Library; **p7** (t) © K. Preston-Mafham/Premaphotos Wildlife; **p8** (b) © H. Fox/Oxford Scientific Films; **p9** (t) © T. Zurowski/CORBIS; (b) © A. Shay/CORBIS; **p10** (t) © L. Sivell/CORBIS; **p10-11** © S. Dalton/Natural History Photographic Agency; **p12** (t) © K. Preston-Mafham/Premaphotos Wildlife; (bl) © R. Preston-Mafham/Premaphotos Wildlife; (br) © K. Preston-Mafham/Premaphotos Wildlife; **p13** (r) © G. Lacz/Frank Lane Picture Agency; **p14** (tr) © S. Dalton/Natural History Photographic Agency; (b) © K. Schafer/CORBIS; **p15** (m) © A. Bannister/CORBIS; **p16** (t) © M. Bowler/Natural History Photographic Agency; (b) © K. Preston-Mafham/Premaphotos Wildlife; **p17** (tr) © R. Planck/Natural History Photographic Agency; (ml) © K. Wilson/CORBIS; (mr) © S. Dalton/Natural History Photographic Agency; (bl) © J. Shaw/Natural History Photographic Agency; **p18** (t) © H. Pfletschinger/Still Pictures; **p19** (t) © R. Pickett/CORBIS; (b) © H. Pfletschinger/Still Pictures; **p20** (t) © A. Bannister/CORBIS; (b) © K. Preston-Mafham/Premaphotos Wildlife; **p21** (t) © A. Bannister/CORBIS; **p22** (l) © K. Preston-Mafham/Premaphotos Wildlife; **p23** (t) © L. Richardson/CORBIS; **p24–25** background © P. Hulme/CORBIS; **p24** (b) © M. Tweedie/Natural History Photographic Agency; **p25** (t) © M. & P. Fogden/CORBIS; (b) © C. Nuridsany & M. Perennou/Science Photo Library; **p26–27** background © Digital Vision; **p26** (tr) © H. Eisenbeiss/Science Photo Library; (m) © S. Dalton/Natural History Photographic Agency; (b) © H. Pfletschinger/Still Pictures; **p27** (t) © Silvestris/Frank Lane Picture Agency; (b) © D. Dominique/Still Pictures; **p28** (r) © F. Grehan/CORBIS; **p29** (tr) © A. Bannister/CORBIS; (b) © A. Bannister/CORBIS; **p30** (l) © G. Lepp/CORBIS; **p31** (tl) © C. Nuridsany & M. Perennou/Science Photo Library; (bl) © N. Dennis/Corbis; (br) © J. Burton/Bruce Coleman; **p32** (tr) © L. Lewis/Frank Lane Picture Agency; (bl) © R. Pickett/CORBIS; **p33** (b) © G. Carter/CORBIS; **p34** (tr) © S. Dalton/Natural History Photographic Agency; (b) © A. Bannister/Natural History Photographic Agency; **p35** (br) © D. Dennis/Oxford Scientific Films; **p36** (tr) © J. Harron/CORBIS; **p36-37** (b) © W. Kaehler/CORBIS; **p37** (t) © P. Marazzi/CORBIS; **p38** (t) © D. Suzio/Science Photo Library; (b) © R. Pickett/CORBIS; **p39** (t) © K. Taylor/Bruce Coleman; (br) © C. Nuridsany & M. Perennou/Science Photo Library; **p40** (l) © K. Preston-Mafham/Premaphotos Wildlife; **p41** (tl) © A. Bannister/Natural History Photographic Agency; (r) © H. & V. Ingen/Natural History Photographic Agency; **p42** (l) © N. Miller/CORBIS; (br) © A. Bannister/CORBIS; **p43** (tr) © P. Goetgheluck/Science Photo Library; (br) © M. Pole/CORBIS; **p44–45** background © Digital Stock; **p44** (tr) © W. Kaehler/CORBIS; (bm) © M. Read/Science Photo Library; **p45** (bm) © M. & P. Fogden/CORBIS; all fact boxes © Digital Vision

With thanks to U.S. expert Aaron Goodwin. Photographic manipulation by John Russell. Managing designer: Mary Cartwright. Managing editor: Jane Chisholm.

Using the Internet ....

Throughout this book we have recommended websites where you can find out more about bugs. To visit the sites, go to the **Usborne Quicklinks Website** where you will find links to all the sites.

1. Go to www.usborne-quicklinks.com
2. Type the keywords for this book: **discovery bugs**
3. Type the page number of the link you want to visit.
4. Click on the link to go to the recommended site.

Here are some of the things you can do on the websites recommended in this book:
- Create your own bugs online
- Watch videos of insects as they hunt their prey
- Search for bugs that live under a rotting log
- See amazing close-up pictures of bugs taken with an electron microscope

Site availability

The links in Usborne Quicklinks are regularly reviewed and updated, but occasionally you may get a message that a site is unavailable. This might be temporary, so try again later, or even the next day. Websites do occasionally close down and when this happens, we will replace them with new links in Usborne Quicklinks. Sometimes we add extra links too, if we think they are useful. So when you visit Usborne Quicklinks, the links may be slightly different from those described in your book.

Downloadable pictures

Pictures marked with a * in this book can be downloaded from the Usborne Quicklinks Website. These pictures are for personal use only and must not be used for commercial purposes.

> COMPUTER NOT ESSENTIAL
> If you don't have access to the Internet, don't worry. This book is a fun and informative introduction to bugs on its own.

Safety on the Internet

Ask your parent's or guardian's permission before you connect to the Internet and make sure you follow these simple rules:

- Never give out information about yourself, such as your real name, address, phone number or the name of your school.
- If a site asks you to log in or register by typing your name or email address, ask permission from an adult first.

What you need

To visit the websites you need a computer with an Internet connection and a web browser (the software that lets you look at information from the Internet). Some sites need extra programs (plug-ins) to play sound or show videos or animations.

If you go to a site and do not have the necessary plug-in, a message will come up on the screen. There is usually a link to click on to download the plug-in. For more information about plug-ins, go to Usborne Quicklinks and click on "Net Help".

Notes for parents and guardians

The websites described in this book are regularly reviewed, but the content of a website may change at any time and Usborne Publishing is not responsible for the content on any website other than its own.

We recommend that children are supervised while on the Internet, that they do not use Internet chat rooms, and that you use Internet filtering software to block unsuitable material. Please ensure that your children read and follow the safety guidelines printed above. For more information, see the Net Help area on the Usborne Quicklinks Website.

Index

Words with several pages sometimes have a number in **bold** to show where to find the main explanation. Page numbers in *italic* show where to find pictures.